STRATHTAY
SCOTTISH BUSES

DAVID DEVOY

AMBERLEY

First published 2019

Amberley Publishing
The Hill, Stroud
Gloucestershire, GL5 4EP

www.amberley-books.com

Copyright © David Devoy, 2019

The right of David Devoy to be identified as
the Author of this work has been asserted in
accordance with the Copyrights, Designs and
Patents Act 1988.

ISBN 978 1 4456 9127 5 (print)
ISBN 978 1 4456 9128 2 (ebook)

British Library Cataloguing in Publication Data.
A catalogue record for this book is available from
the British Library.

Typesetting by Aura Technology and Software
Services, India. Printed in the UK.

Introduction

The Scottish Bus Group (SBG) was a state-owned group of bus operators covering the whole of mainland Scotland. The origin of the grouping was the operators owned by the Scottish Motor Traction company after Nationalisation in 1948 under the control of the British Transport Commission. Highland Omnibuses was added to the group in 1952. A new holding company, Scottish Omnibuses Group (Holdings), was formed in 1961, and this was renamed the Scottish Bus Group in 1963. Meanwhile, the group had come under control of the Transport Holding Company in 1962 when the British Transport Commission was wound up. It went on to become part of the Scottish Transport Group on 1 January 1969.

However, the industry was changing and express coach services were deregulated by the Transport Act 1980 under the Thatcher government five years before the deregulation of local bus services by the Transport Act 1985. The SBG also had to deal with local authorities when financial aid was required to keep local bus services running. It made sense to alter the bus company areas to coincide with the relevant local authorities. The SBG announced in October 1984 that major changes were on the way. Additional new companies were formed, and Strathtay Scottish was set up in March 1985 to operate the eastern operations of Alexanders (Midland) based in Perth, Crieff and Pitlochry, as well as the southern operations of Alexanders (Northern) in Dundee, Forfar, Arbroath, Blairgowrie and Montrose. A bright blue and orange livery was adopted for the fleet, which would be controlled from Dundee. Andrew Gall was to be appointed as general manager.

Monday 17 June was launch day, but the new colour schemes was unveiled at Buchanan bus station in Glasgow on 12 June. Strathtay sent along Olympian TSO 25X. The fleet numbering system adopted included separate classes for different type of vehicles. Sixty-three buses were transferred from Northern Scottish, joined by a further sixty-three from Midland Scottish. One early repaint was SL10, out-shopped with a Gaelic version of the fleet name, Strathtaha Albanach, but this was not repeated. Stickers were applied over the old fleet names, until repaints occurred. No depot allocation plates were carried.

Locally, the independent A&C McLennan of Spittalfield was taken over by Stagecoach of Perth in November 1985. An insight into the future occurred when two rear-entrance AEC Routemasters were borrowed from Clydeside Scottish for use in Perth and Dundee to test their suitability, and twenty examples were ordered.

Greyhound of Arbroath and Strathtay both registered Arbroath local services, but in the event Greyhound withdrew from stage-carriage work, leaving the field clear for Strathtay. Stagecoach registered Perth's first-ever night service, along with services between Perth, Pitlochry and Aberfeldy.

These were taken over by Stagecoach from Strathtay in August, and were actually operated on hire to Strathtay until deregulation day on 26 October. In Dundee, Tayside Regional Council did not register many of the existing joint services, or any routes at the outer end of Perth Road. These were quickly covered by Strathtay and operated as 'Tayway'. This allowed a network of cross-town routes to be established. Highwayman of Errol launched some shopper's services, and Docherty of Auchterarder won the tender for the Perth to Stirling service. White waistbands began to be added to the livery, which brightened it up. Express coach services were operated by the company for Scottish Citylink, which received some coaches from other SBG companies to upgrade the fleet. Also received were some inherited orders outstanding from both Midland and Northern Scottish.

Many older buses were leaving the fleet, including Fleetlines and Fords, while more Routemasters were purchased. The Nationals were transferred to Northern Scottish and replaced by some ex-Manchester Fleetlines and Northern Tigers. Pitlochry depot was closed and advertised for sale, and many Perth services were revised. Many second-hand Leopards were taken into stock to replace older manual-gearbox buses. A new, much bolder coach livery was introduced to entice more private hires. A batch of Leyland Olympians were purchased from Fife Scottish and pressed into service, but were soon refurbished. 1988 also saw the beginning of a fleet of odd minibuses, purchased for school contracts. This head office was moved from Whitehall Crescent to Seagate bus station in Dundee. A strange event occurred when Fleetline SD11 was lent to Irvine's of Law between September and October. This was explained by the fact that the company had taken over some supermarket contracts from Highwayman of Errol, and had taken a pair of Volvo Ailsas as part of the deal. These were resold immediately to Irvine's, but one was defective and so was briefly replaced by the Fleetline. A start was made to repaint the Routemasters out of the diagonal style of livery into a more subdued version.

When Smith of Coupar Angus started to compete on the Blairgowrie to Perth corridor with reduced fares in 1989, Strathtay took an unusual course of action: it created a fictional independent named Mackays Coaches and repainted three coaches into a blue, orange and white colour scheme with no reference to Strathtay Scottish and matched the fares offered by Smith's. This looked as if three companies were now operating on the route, confusing passengers. Elsewhere Wishart of Friockheim ran to Brechin, Meffan's of Kirriemuir in the Forfar area and Bean's of Brechin competed between Montrose and Brechin. At this time Strathtay ran 157 buses, fifty-eight being OMO double-deckers and twenty-five crew-operated Routemasters. The rest were single-deckers and minibuses. The average age was ten years old, dragged down by the elderly Routemaster fleet.

The mighty Stagecoach Group announced in May 1989 its intention to compete in Perth on the lucrative city services. This would be under the name of 'Perth Panther' and was launched in June, but Strathtay responded by repainting six Routemasters into 'Perth City Transport' red and cream livery. Strathtay had lost its managing director, Neil Renilson, to Stagecoach earlier and this undermined the company when it was in the throes of privatisation. Stagecoach was relentless and registered more and more services over the coming months. Tayside Public Transport Co. was also being privatised through an employee/management buyout, so Strathtay was under threat on many fronts at the same time. Stagecoach announced the sale of its express coach services, to prevent any conflict of interest in bidding for Scottish Bus Group subsidiaries in the forthcoming privatisation process. Strathtay was also hindered by the privatisation process as it could not access new buses since the SBG was not allowing purchases at this time. Special dispensation was reluctantly granted to allow for the purchase of thirteen new minibuses for repelling the Stagecoach incursion into Perth. Strathtay services were also registered on the former A&C McLennan routes against Stagecoach. The Mackays Coaches services were cancelled however, as the resources were needed elsewhere.

1990 saw an uneasy co-existence between Strathtay with Magicbus Scotland, as Stagecoach had renamed itself after the express coach services were sold to the National Express group. Further second-hand buses joined the company from other SBG fleets. The company was officially put on the market in November, with 168 buses, 7 depots and 436 staff involved. Changes by Tayside Buses brought some extra work for Strathtay in the Broughty Ferry area. Stagecoach was announced as the successful bidder for Northern Scottish, which adjoined Strathtay territory to the north. Local independent Greyhound Luxury Coaches was acquired by Tayside Public Transport on 13 August 1990, being rebranded Tayside Greyhound.

The takeover occurred in June 1991 after it was announced that Yorkshire Traction was preferred bidder for Strathtay. It is believed that their bid was only just ahead of that submitted by the Strathtay management and employees by a few thousand pounds. No other bidders made a final offer. Despite experiencing heavy and sustained competition on the lucrative city services in Perth, Strathtay Scottish managed to remain profitable on the run up to privatisation, and in June 1991 was sold to Barnsley-based Yorkshire Traction Ltd for £1.11 million. Now trading simply as Strathtay Buses, the new owners established and maintained a working relationship with Stagecoach around Perth, even jointly operating the trunk service between Dundee and Perth with the national operator, while the remainder of the operations remained largely unchanged from privatisation. June saw Tayside Buses sold to the management/employees for £4 million. Fife Scottish had also passed to the Stagecoach Group around this time, so Strathtay was bordered all around by firms under new ownership. Crieff depot was closed in August after a loss of contracts and service reductions west of Perth. As would be expected, second-hand buses tended to come from other companies in the Yorkshire Traction Group. The Perth City Transport identity was abandoned in favour of fleet livery. A new departure for the fleet was the re-bodying of older buses with new East Lancs bodies.

Five new Dennis Darts were ordered for services in the Arbroath area in 1992, for delivery the following year. Routemasters were also being phased out, although the services continued to be crew-operated. The entire fleet was renumbered into a single numerical scheme in March 1993. The company could not sustain the level of intense competition that ensued around Perth, and in 1993 it closed its depot after staff rejected proposed new pay and working conditions. On a brighter note, the fifteen-vehicle fleet of Meffan's of Kirriemuir was added to the Yorkshire Traction portfolio in October 1993. Tayside Buses purchased the business of G&N Wishart of Friockheim during the year.

The services provided by Bean's of Brechin were taken over by Strathtay in January 1994. Tayside Regional Council gave its backing for a plan to acquire and demolish Seagate bus station in late May; meanwhile, the Perth depot was vacated on 24 June, and sold for redevelopment. 1995 continued with investment in new vehicles with Northern Counties-bodied Darts and Olympians. 1996 witnessed further Darts and Optare MetroRiders being purchased. Some buses in the Dundee area were fitted with cash vaults for use on evening services.

In February 1997 Tayside Buses was sold to National Express and rebranded Travel Dundee, adding financial muscle to its major rival in the area. More new Darts were obtained for Strathtay in 1997, this time for Montrose depot. These were joined by three new Volvo coaches for Scottish Citylink work, and some second-hand MCW Metroriders from Yorkshire. A huge investment was announced in January 1998 when an order was placed for eight new Volvo Olympians fitted with East Lancs Pyoneer bodies. Dundee's new bus station opened on 24 July. It was a joint project between Strathtay Scottish, Dundee City Council and Scottish Enterprise and cost £680,000. 1999 witnessed the purchase of four Mercedes Varios, which, along with MCW Metroriders transferred from Yorkshire, enabled many older buses to be withdrawn. A new service started in April was the 100, which linked Dundee and the airport. October brought in four new East Lancs-bodied Dennis Darts to upgrade the fleet. Six Leyland Tigers were rebodied with East Lancs Millenium bodies in 2000 to replace Leyland Leopards on interurban routes. Another new service in Dundee was launched when the 73 linked the city centre to The Glens.

A new source of second-hand buses was tapped in 2001 when Stagecoach supplied some Leyland Tigers from its Bluebird and Fife subsidiaries. After trying demonstration vehicles, the first low-floor double-deckers were ordered by the company and the Volvo B7TL chassis was coupled with East Lancs Vyking bodywork. Some MetroRiders were also obtained from the defunct Tillingbourne of Cranleigh fleet, and these were repainted at Barnsley prior to delivery. 2002 saw another five Volvo B7TL deckers ordered for delivery in November, while a further order for delivery in April 2003 was placed later. Two Mercedes Varios were also ordered for October delivery.

2004 began with the order of a low-floor Optare Solo for the Blairgowrie/Carsie service. This received funding from Perth and Kinross Council and arrived in April. Further second-hand acquisitions were Mercedes Varios from Yorkshire Traction and Volvo B10Bs from the Blazefield Group. The year ended with an announcement by the Scottish Parliament stating that a free, unrestricted Scotland-wide free bus travel scheme for people over sixty, and those with disabilities, would come into force in April 2005.

2005 began with an order being placed for four new Volvo B7TL double-deckers and a batch of Optare Solos. A new Iveco Daily entered service at Dundee depot in January. Further Volvo B10Bs were also purchased from Blazefield to upgrade the fleet. Funds were secured from Angus Council to improve services around Forfar, while Dundee Council funded improvements to cross-city travel. The company took over operations of service 29 from Nicoll of Laurencekirk, and services 115/6 from Petrie of Forfar. Things seemed to be going better than ever for Strathtay when the bombshell struck.

On 14 December 2005, Strathtay Buses' parent company, Traction Group, was purchased by Stagecoach for £26 million. The deal was paid with £21.4 million in cash and £4.5 million in shares, and Stagecoach also took over the Traction Group's £11 million of debt. Strathtay was bordered to the north, east and south by Stagecoach subsidiaries, all part of Stagecoach East Scotland, which Strathtay had also joined. The Stagecoach corporate livery was adopted for vehicles and, initially, most displayed 'Strathtay – Part of the Stagecoach Group' fleet names; however, all buses have been repainted or replaced, so they no longer carry any reference to Strathtay. In 2013 the company licence was transferred to Stagecoach Fife. As such, another part of the Scottish bus scene has been confined to history.

Thanks to my good friend Alistair Scobbie for his help, and for allowing me to use a few of his photographs. Thanks as ever to my two daughters, Samantha and Jennifer, for their help with proofreading and technical support.

JSS 201V was a Ford R1014/Alexander Y Type B45F new as Northern Scottish NT 201 in August 1980. A total of 273 Fords were produced with this style of bodywork. It passed to Strathtay Scottish in June 1985 as its SF21, and was arriving in Dundee, still in its former livery but with amended fleet names, when seen. On disposal in October 1987 it was purchased by Wiles of Port Seton, passing to Glass of Haddington in December 1989 and into the Lowland Omnibuses fleet with that business. It then worked for Mayne's of Buckie, Wheeler of Catshill and Harrington of Coventry.

NMS 587M was a Leyland Leopard PSU3/3R/Alexander Y Type B53F new as Alexander (Midland) MPE 187 in October 1973, and allocated to Perth depot. It became Strathtay SL6 and is shown in its home depot with Strathtay titles on the side but with Midland still on the front. It would take time to merge the two constituent fleets. This bus would remain in the fleet until 1987. The company would employ seventy Leyland Leopard chassis with a mixture of body styles.

SCS 341M was a Leyland Leopard PSU3/3R/Alexander Y Type C49F new as Western SMT L2472 in July 1974. It was transferred to Highland Scottish as its L56 before passing to Midland Scottish as its MPE 426, and then to Strathtay Scottish as its fleet number SL50 in November 1985. It was captured here in Aberdeen. It would see further service with Merideth of Malpas in October 1987, then Wright's of Wrexham in December.

CRS 72T was a Leyland Leopard PSU3E/4R/Duple Dominant C49F new as Northern Scottish NPE 72 in August 1979. It was allocated to Arbroath depot, and became Strathtay property in June 1985. It was allocated fleet number SL27, and was re-registered as 691 DYE in December 1987. It was re-registered yet again in April 1992 as ASP 218T, and renumbered as 527 in the following March. This view shows it in Newcastle, preparing for a journey to Edinburgh.

In 1977 Alexander (Midland) allocated a batch of Alexander-bodied Volvo Ailsa B55-10s to its Perth depot. YMS 703R received fleet number MRA3, and passed to Strathtay as its V3 with four others in June 1985. They later moved to Dundee in late 1989, but only lasted until December 1990, when they were sold to Kelvin Central Buses. This one received fleet number 1981 and remained in service until March 1995, before going to Dunsmore (dealer) of Larkhall for scrap.

B334 LSO was a Leyland Tiger TRCTL11/2RP/Alexander TE Type C47F new as Northern Scottish NCT 34 in January 1985. It was only in the fleet for around five months before being transferred to Strathtay Scottish as its ST12. It received Scottish Citylink colours in December 1986, but lost them around two years later when it was repainted into Strathtay coach livery. It was re-registered as WLT 427 in 1991, and renumbered as 412 the following year. It would pass to Stagecoach with the business and was allocated fleet number 59069.

NMS 559M was a Leyland Leopard PSU3/3R/Alexander Y Type B53F new as Alexander
(Midland) MPE159 in August 1973. It received Strathtay fleet number SL47 and was given this
unusual version of the livery, which was basically the old Midland livery with the cream painted
over in orange. Happily the idea wasn't perpetuated as it tended to look rather drab. It was
sitting outside Perth depot on a chilly winter morning when seen. This bus later passed to both
Meridas of Malpas and Wright's of Wrexham but did not enter service.

LMS 156W was a Leyland Fleetline FE30 AGR/Alexander AD Type H44/31F new as Midland
Scottish MRF 156 in August 1980. It was transferred to Strathtay Scottish in June 1985 and
was snapped in Perth. It would become number 715 and be re-registered as WGB 711W in
August 1993. Twenty-two Fleetlines were operated by the company, with bodywork provided
by Alexander, Eastern Coachworks and Northern Counties.

NMS 564M was a Leyland Leopard PSU3/3R/Alexander Y Type B53F new as Alexander (Midland) MPE 164 in August 1973. It passed to Strathtay as its SL48, and was laying over in Dundee between duties when seen. It left the fleet in October 1987 and passed to Merideth of Malpas, then Norman of Keynsham, Byegone Buses of Biddenden, Golden Coaches of Llantwit Major, Brewer's of Caerau, and Davies Bros of Pencader.

BMS 512Y was a Leyland Tiger TRBTL11/2R/Alexander TE Type C49F new as Alexander (Midland) MPT 112 in April 1983, and allocated to Perth depot. It would pass to Strathtay as its ST7 in 1985, and was re-registered as VLT 298 in May 1988. It was renumbered as 407 in March 1993, and re-registered as 866 PYC in November 2001. It was upseated to DP60F at this time. It received Stagecoach fleet number 59070 in 2006 and was re-registered as PES 463Y on disposal. It then went south to join the fleet of Wootens/Tiger Line and became BIG 4269 in 2011. It later worked for Javelin Coaches of Basingstoke before returning to Scotland with John Carson's WJC fleet.

NLS 986W was a Leyland National NL116L11/1R B52F new as Midland Scottish MPN 34 in December 1980. It was transferred with Perth depot in 1985, and became Strathtay SN6. Eleven Nationals were inherited by the company, but had a short life. This one passed to Northern Scottish in May 1987, where it was numbered NPN16. It moved again in December 1989 to Fife Scottish as its fleet number 386. It would last into Stagecoach days and received the 'stripes' livery in 1992.

SUS 265W was a Ford 'A Series'/Alexander (Belfast) B27F purchased new by Central Scottish as its FS3 in 1980. It passed to Clydeside Scottish as its L365 in August 1987, before resale to Strathtay Scottish as its SS3 in July 1988. It was always either over a pit or in bits whenever I saw it. It later passed to Malloch of Burrleton and Hall's of Kennoway. The A series was introduced in 1973 as a range of trucks built by Ford UK to bridge the gap between the relatively small 3.5-ton GVW Transit and the bigger 7-ton D series.

As an experiment, a pair of crew-operated AEC Routemasters were borrowed from Clydeside Scottish in November and December 1985. It was deemed as a success and a batch was obtained directly from London Transport. WLT 921 was new as RM921 in November 1961 and carried a Park Royal H36/28R body. SR8 arrived in September 1986 and was re-registered as YTS 892A around a year later. It was snapped in Dundee in the early version of Strathtay livery, but this was later modified.

SCS 363M was a Leyland Leopard PSU3/3R/Alexander Y Type C49F new as SMT L2494 in February 1975. It passed to Strathtay in June 1985 as its SL10 and was allocated to Perth depot. These early Leopards were manual gearbox buses and were proving to be quite unsuitable for use in urban areas. Still with a few years of life left in them, however, they were deemed to be useful in more rural areas, where fewer stops had to be made.

SSJ 135Y was a Leyland Tiger TRCTL11/3R/Duple Goldliner C46Ft purchased new by Western Scottish as its L135 in December 1982. It was not destined to stay long however, and passed to Strathtay as its ST14 in 1986. It was captured in Glasgow while working for Scottish Citylink. It was re-registered as WLT 943 in April 1988 and on disposal in November 1990 became PSN 916Y. It later worked for Morris Travel of Pencoed and Beardsmore of Rudheath.

XMS 243R was a Leyland Leopard PSU3C/3R/Alexander Y Type B53F new as Alexander (Midland) MPE 243 in March 1977. It passed to Strathtay Scottish in June 1985, and was caught in Perth. It later became a driver trainer. This batch was diverted from a Western SMT order, and featured long-bay side windows. On disposal it passed to the Scottish Vintage Bus Museum as a source of spare parts.

G892 FJW was a Renault S56/Dormobile B25F delivered new as Strathtay Scottish SS9 in August 1989. It was delivered in Perth City Transport red and cream in an effort to repel an attack by Stagecoach in the area. It was later given standard colours as shown by this view taken in Perth. It was withdrawn in 1999. This was part of a batch of thirteen purchased from the stock of the Carlyle Bus Centre after special dispensation was given by Scottish Bus Group headquarters as privatisation was ongoing at the time.

XMS 251R was a Leyland Leopard PSU3C/3R/Alexander B53F new as Alexander (Midland) MPE251 in March 1977. It still carried its old livery, complete with 'bluebird' transfer, when snapped in Perth bus station. The seating had been changed to dual-purpose specification at some point. In the early days there only seemed to be one size of Strathtay fleet name available, causing many buses to have the side names changed, but with the old name on the front retained.

A126 ESG was a Leyland Tiger TRCTL11/3RH/Duple Laser C46Ft new as Midland Scottish MPT 126 in June 1984. It was delivered in Scottish Citylink livery, but was transferred to Strathtay as its ST8 just one year later. It was re-registered as VLT 42 in January 1988, then A651 XGG in December 1990. This was changed to FSU 309 in January 1991, and the bus received fleet number 408 in March 1993. It was upseated to C55F in 1996, and re-registered back to A651 XGG on disposal in 2001.

D310 MHS was a Dodge S56/Alexander B21F new as Central Scottish R10 in October 1986. It was lent to Kelvin Scottish/KCB as its number 1010 in 1989, and was then sold to Northern Scottish in February 1990 as its NM10. On disposal in June 1992 it passed to Dewvale (t/a Bellview Coaches) of Paisley, but in a strange quirk of fate was accepted by Strathtay as a trade-in against three surplus Routemasters. It joined Strathtay as SS29 and was reunited with other members from the same batch purchased directly from KCB. It received this advert for KOKO's Amusement Centres in November 1992.

D30 SAO was a Dodge S56/Reebur B23F new as Cumberland number 30 in October 1986. It was purchased by Strathtay in August 1993, and is shown at Forfar depot with fleet number 133. It was later transferred to the associated Meffan of Kirriemuir operation and upseated to B27F. On disposal it passed to McCreadie's of Airdrie and remained there until 1998, when it passed to Dunsmore of Larkhall for scrap.

RRS 54R was a Leyland Leopard PSU3E/4R/Duple Dominant Express C49F new as Alexander (Northern) NPE 54 in March 1977. It passed to Strathtay in June 1985 as its number SL20, and was resting outside Montrose depot. It gained 'Mackays Coaches' livery in November 1988 as an anti-competitive measure against Smith's of Coupar Angus, and was re-registered as 365 DXU. It later returned to the main fleet and was renumbered as 520. It was re-registered as PSR 119R on disposal.

XMS 248R was a Leyland Leopard PSU3C/3R/Alexander Y Type B53F new as Alexander (Midland) MPE 248 in March 1977. As it was allocated to Crieff depot, it passed to Strathtay Scottish in June 1985, and was allocated fleet number SL17. It was renumbered as 92 in 1993 and soldiered on for another couple of years, before passing to the Scottish Vintage Bus Museum for spares.

TSO 25X was a Leyland Olympian ONLXB/1R/ECW H45/32F new as Northern Scottish NLO 25 in March 1982. It became Strathtay Scottish SO7 in June 1985, and is shown in Dundee, complete with 'Best Bus' decals. It would later be renumbered as 907. It passed to sister company Roadcar in March 1999 and was allocated fleet number 625.

A112 ESA was a Leyland Tiger TRBTL11/2R/Alexander P Type B52F new as Northern Scottish NBT 12 in September 1983. The rather box-like bodywork was designed for the Singapore bus market. It was one of four transferred to Strathtay in exchange for Leyland Nationals in March 1987. Numbered SBT1, it was allocated to Perth depot. It was renumbered as 501 in March 1993 and was given this advertising livery for the Venue Nightclub in June 1993. It ran like this for one year before regaining fleet livery.

BSG 546W was a Leyland Tiger TRCTL11/3R/Duple Dominant III C46Ft new as Eastern Scottish XH 546 in July 1981. It passed to Midland Scottish and Kelvin Scottish before reaching Strathtay as its ST17 in July 1986. In October 1987 it was rebuilt to Dominant IV style and was re-registered as 17 CLT. By December 1989 this was changed to XDS 685W, then 821 DYE the following year. At the end of 1991 it had the bodywork stripped off and was dispatched to East Lancs in Blackburn, to be fitted with this new DP57F body as shown in Dundee.

ULS 330T was a Leyland Leopard PSU3E/4R/Alexander Y Type B53F new as Midland Scottish MPE 330 in April 1979. It became Strathtay Scottish SL31 in June 1985, and was allocated to Perth depot. The fleet number was changed to 531 in March 1993, as seen here in Dundee. It was transferred to the associated Meffan's of Kirriemuir fleet in October 1993. It then passed through various preservationists hands and will hopefully be returned to Midland livery in due course.

The Scottish Bus Group specified special coaches for its London services. These featured small double-glazed trapezoid windows, but when the coaches came up for disposal a poor price was obtained as they were not suitable for general coach work. A solution was tried when some Duple Dominant IIIs were rebuilt to Dominant IV specification, using much larger side windows. ST17 shows the results as it sits in Dundee bus station.

HGA 983D was a Bedford VAS1/Willowbrook B24FM purchased new by MacBraynes of Glasgow as its number 210 in May 1966. In 1972 it was transferred to Highland Omnibuses as its CD93. Strathtay Scottish purchased it in 1988 from the Highland Health Board, and it is seen in Forfar as its number SS1. The idea was that office and admin staff could cover school contracts with elderly buses each morning and afternoon with little outlay. This bus survives in preservation as a MacBraynes bus once again.

LJA 481P was a Daimler Fleetline CRG6LXB/Northern Counties H43/32F new as Greater Manchester PTE number 7481 in February 1976. Six of these buses were purchased by Strathtay Scottish in March 1987 as part of a deal to replace Leyland Nationals in the fleet. SD21 was captured in Dundee city centre as it headed for Tayport on service 72. It would later be renumbered as 721.

VLT 26 was an AEC Routemaster R2RH/Park Royal H36/28R new as Transport RM26 in November 1959. These elderly buses were seen as an attractive proposition to re-introduce conductors on the Tayway corridor. They were cheap to buy and very reliable. SR21 was leaving the stance at Arbroath to head back into Dundee when seen. In March 1990 the bus was re-registered as XSL 220A, and three years later it was renumbered as 621. It would see further service with Reading Mainline from June 1994 onwards.

JLS 764S was a Ford R1014/Duple Dominant C45F new as Alexander (Midland) MT64 in July 1978. Midland operated coach tours, and these vehicles were purchased with a bus grant, which meant that 50 per cent of their mileage had to be on bus services. JLS 764S passed to Strathtay Scottish as its SF11 in June 1985 and received this livery, which used cream instead of white. It was snapped on the forecourt of Perth depot.

E414 GES was an MCW Metrobus DR102/60/Alexander RL Type H47/33F new as Strathtay Scottish SM14 in August 1987. The livery was changed in August 1988 to this version, complete with large 'Strathtay Coaches' fleet names, despite the fact that normal bus seats were fitted. It was renumbered as 814 and re-registered as YJU 694 in December 1993, and actually did receive coach seats on the lower deck in 1997. It would remain with the fleet into Stagecoach days as its number 15894 and it is seen here arriving in Perth.

D307 MHS was a Dodge S56/Alexander B21F new as Central Scottish R7 in October 1986. It passed to Kelvin Scottish in May 1989 as its fleet number 1007, before becoming Strathtay SS19 in March 1990. It was renumbered as 119 in March 1993, and is shown working the Arbroath town service. It would pass to sister company Lincolnshire Roadcar in March 1995 as their number 107.

VSS 4X was a Leyland Tiger TRCTL11/3R/Duple Goldliner III C46Ft new as Northern Scottish NLT4 in July 1982 for use on the London service. It passed to Strathtay Scottish in 1985, and received Scottish Citylink colours around one year later. It was rebuilt to Goldliner IV style and re-registered as WLT 743 in 1988. In May 1992 it was given a new East Lancs body and lasted in service until 2004.

ULS 633X was an MCW Metrobus DR102/28/Alexander RL Type H45/33F new as Midland Scottish MRM33 in May 1982. Eight of these buses passed to Strathtay Scottish on its formation with a further three on order. This batch were moved to Dundee after the closure of Perth depot, and 805 is seen in the city centre, bound for Ninewells Hospital. It received a full repaint in 1989, when the white band was added.

DMS 368C was a Leyland Leopard PSU3/3R/Alexander Y Type C49F new as Alexander (Midland) MPE82 in September 1965. It was cut down as a tow-wagon and passed to Strathtay in 1985. After the use of trade plates was discontinued it was given the registration number Q739PES, and is shown at Dundee depot. These manual-gearbox buses made ideal tow-wagons and were used throughout the Scottish Bus Group.

D315 SGB was a Leyland Tiger TRCTL11/3RZ/Duple 340 C49Ft new to Central Scottish as its fleet number C15 in May 1987. It passed to Kelvin Central in 1989 and carried Scottish Citylink livery. Its stay would be brief however, as Citylink work was deemed to be unprofitable. It moved to Strathtay Scottish in 1990 as ST25, and later became WLT 943 (fleet number 425). It was rebodied by East Lancs with a Millennium 2000 body, and later passed to Woottens/ Tiger Line, McCree of Shepshed and Ogden of St Helens as B11 WTN, KIG 1373 and AAL 520A respectively.

WLT 759 was an AEC Routemaster R2RH/Park Royal H36/28R new as London Transport RM759 in April 1961. It passed to Strathtay in July 1986 as its SR3, and was re-registered as WTS 329A in June 1989. At the same time the company resurrected the old Perth City Transport colours in an attempt to keep the mighty Stagecoach at bay. The corporation bus fleet had been taken over by Alexanders in 1934, and the livery was used locally until 1961.

I first came across the fictitious 'McKays Coaches' on a visit to Buckie depot, when three coaches were in storage, well out of the way. Their fleet numbers were SL20/8/68. The idea was that it would look like a small independent operator. Smith's of Coupar Angus had registered a service between Perth and Blairgowrie to compete with established Strathtay service. MacKays was there to confuse passengers into believing that two independents were competing on the route. WLT 316 had begun life as Midland Scottish ULS 650T, and was a Leyland Leopard PSU3E/4R/Duple Dominant II C49F purchased new in March 1979 as MPE 343. It was transferred to Kelvin Scottish in June 1985, and moved to Strathtay in 1988, where it was re-registered as WLT 316. The competition on the route quickly faded and the raison d'être for MacKays soon evaporated.

C243 OFE was a Mercedes L608D/Reebur B20F new as Lincolnshire Roadcar number 43 in July 1986. As both companies were members of the Yorkshire Traction Group, it was transferred to Strathtay in January 1995, and is shown in Perth. It would give almost ten years of service in Scotland. Reeve Burgess was a bus body manufacturer based in Pilsley, north-east Derbyshire, but more people referred to it as Reebur. It was a subsidiary of Plaxton from 1980 until its closure in 1991.

D309 DSR was an MCW Metrobus DR102/52/Alexander RL Type H45/33F new as Strathtay Scottish SM9 in August 1986, and had been an outstanding order place by Midland before the new company's formation. It received 'coach style' livery in August 1988, and was caught in Perth. It was given coach seats in January 2001. Production of the Metrobus ceased in 1989 with the financial collapse of MCW.

A114 ESA was a Leyland Tiger TRBTL11/2R/Alexander P Type B52F new as Northern Scottish NBT14 in September 1983. Alexander's long history of producing attractive and well-rounded designs came to an abrupt halt with the P Type. It might have been sturdy and practical, with flat glass used extensively, but it would never win any beauty contests. Happily, it later morphed into the PS Type, which became the standard bus for the Stagecoach Group.

D316 SGB was a Leyland Tiger TRCTL11/3RZ/Duple 340 C49Ft new as Central Scottish C16 in May 1987. It was on loan to Kelvin Scottish for a spell before purchase by Strathtay in May 1990. It was based at Perth and received fleet number ST26, before being re-registered as WLT 759 at the end of the year. It then became D841 COS, before becoming 365 DXU in 1993. It received this livery in 1995, and was seen here in Glasgow.

C111 BTS was a Leyland Olympian ONLXB/1RV/Alexander RL Type H47/32F new as Strathtay Scottish SO11 in July 1986. The company was unusual in purchasing both Metrobuses and Olympians. C111 BTS was renumbered as 911 in March 1993, and was fitted with coach seats in 1998. This view shows it in Dundee while working on service 73, bound for the hospital.

CRS 75T was a Leyland Leopard PSU3E/4R/Duple Dominant C49F new as Alexander (Northern) NPE75 in August 1979. It was transferred to Strathtay Scottish in June 1985 as its number SL28. It received MacKays Coaches livery to combat the Smith's of Coupar Angus Blairgowrie–Perth service, but was later re-deployed on the Pitcairngreen service. The service was withdrawn in January 1991. The bus was renumbered as 528 in 1993, and re-registered as ASP 97T prior to disposal.

SSS 539X was a Mercedes L508D/Reebur C19F purchased new by Mair's of Bucksburn in October 1981. It was acquired by Strathtay Scottish in August 1990 and allocated fleet number SS22, although this was later changed to 122. It was withdrawn in March 1995 and sold to Blair of Guthrie. The company built up a fleet of odd minibuses purchased cheaply to run various school contracts throughout the area.

In 1971 Central SMT took delivery of a fleet of thirty-five Daimler Fleetlines with handsome bodies by ECW. They were suitable for one-man operation, but failed to find favour with Central and were quickly discarded. They entered service with other group subsidiaries. These two were reunited under Strathtay ownership, becoming SD1/2 respectively. Both would receive the orange and blue livery in due course.

A988 FLS was a Leyland Olympian ONLXB/1R/Alexander RL Type H45/32F new as Fife Scottish number 788 in November 1983. It was one of six purchased by Strathtay Scottish in July 1988 and was allocated fleet number S023. Initially it ran in 'as acquired' condition, still in red and cream. It was rebuilt with coach seats and soft trim internally in January 1989, later gaining the registration plate PSU 374 as shown in this view taken in Dundee.

CWG 914L was a Daimler Fleetline CRG6LXB Alexander D Type H75F delivered new to Midland as its MRF 104 in February 1973. It was allocated to Perth depot, but it had quite a short life with its original owner as it was transferred to W. Alexander & Sons (Northern), where it was numbered NRF16 in May 1977 so that OMO could be extended to the double-deck fleet in the far north. It was transferred to Strathtay in June 1985 and was back in Perth, working an early morning school contract, when seen.

A126 ESG was a Leyland Tiger TRCTL11/3RH/Duple Laser C46Ft new as Midland Scottish MPT 126 in June 1984. It became Strathtay Scottish ST8 in June 1985 and retained Citylink livery. It was re-registered as VLT 42 in January 1988, and was captured in Perth. December 1990 saw the registration plate changed to A651 XGG, then FSU309 the following year. The fleet number became 408 in March 1993, and the seating was later changed to C55F.

Seen loading in Perth, K304 MSN was a Dennis Dart 9.8SDL/Wright Handybus B39F new as Strathtay number 304 in April 1993. It was moved from Arbroath to Dundee depot and fitted with a vault to allow its use on Dundee services in the evenings. It passed to Stagecoach as fleet number 32479 in July 2006 with the business and was given route branding for the 'Round O' in Arbroath. It lasted until 2009.

Seen in Dundee on service 73, ST52 NTL was a Volvo B7TL/East Lancs Vyking H47/29F new as Strathtay number 704 in November 2002. These buses provided low-floor access, Hanover LED destination screens and high-backed seats. 704 became Stagecoach 16924 after the company was sold, and later received 'Tayway 73' route branding. The B7TL featured a transversely mounted rear engine, but the radiator was mounted on the right side of the engine compartment. It was equipped with a Volvo D7C engine and a ZF or Voith gearbox.

X645 RDA was a Volvo B7TL/East Lancs Vyking H47/29F built as a demonstrator for Volvo Bus & Coach, Warwick, in October 2000. It was used by Strathtay in 2001 between March and April. It was later sold to JJ Kavanaugh in Eire and re-registered as 00-KE-11, later returning to the UK and working for South Lancs Travel and D&G Buses of Crewe as X80 SLT.

B334 LSO was a Leyland Tiger TRCTL11/2RP/Alexander TE Type C47F new as Northern Scottish NCT34 in January 1985. It was transferred to Strathtay Scottish after just five months and received fleet number ST12. It was re-registered as WLT 427 in August 1991, and renumbered as 412 in the fleet renumbering in March 1993. It would last into Stagecoach ownership, with whom it was allocated fleet number 59069.

E540 VKY was an MCW Metrorider MF150/33 B23F new as Yorkshire Traction fleet number 540 in October 1987. It was transferred to Strathtay as its number 161 in July 1998, and allocated to Dundee depot. It later served at both Montrose and Arbroath depots before withdrawal in 2004. The MCW Metrorider, launched at the 1986 Motor Show, was designed and built by Metro-Cammell Weymann (MCW) between 1986 and 1989. It was an integral bus, marking it out from its van-based rivals of the time.

A986 FLS was a Leyland Olympian ONLXB/1R/Alexander RL Type H45/32F new as Fife Scottish FRO6 in November 1983. It was transferred to Strathtay as its SO21 in July 1988, and was pressed into service in 'as acquired' condition with the fleet names altered, as shown in this view taken in Dundee. It was rebuilt to coach spec using refurbished seats from Alexander Y Types in June 1989, being re-registered as PSU 372.

TSO 18X was a Leyland Olympian ONLXB/1R/ECW H45/32F new as Northern Scottish NLO18 in February 1982. It was one of a batch of six acquired from Northern on the formation of the new company, and received fleet number S05, and later 905. It is seen in Dundee looking very smart. In August 1998 it passed to sister company Roadcar as its number 618. On disposal in 2004 it was sold to Johnson's of Hodthorpe.

XMS 248R was a Leyland Leopard PSU3C/3R/Alexander Y Type B53F new as Alexander (Midland) MPE248 in March 1977. It became Strathtay SL17, and was based initially at Crieff depot. In later years it received fleet number 92 and was used for driver training, as evident in this view taken in Perth. The Leyland Leopard was a mid-engined chassis manufactured by Leyland between 1959 and 1982. Most Scottish Bus Group examples were fitted with the 11.1-litre O.680 engine and the Leyland part-synchromesh gearbox, coded as PSU3.3R.

VRS 144L was a Daimler Fleetline CRL6-30/Alexander AL Type H45/29D new as Aberdeen Corporation number 144 in March 1973. It passed to Grampian and then Northern Scottish before transfer to Strathtay. It was actually moved to Perth depot before the transfer and ran very briefly as Midland Scottish MRF 144. It became Strathtay SD9, and later passed to Highland Scottish as its K944.

If there was ever an ironic advert on a bus, Strathtay Scottish SO18 carried it. Luckily it must have had an organ donor card, as it was rebuilt and returned to service. It was a Leyland Olympian ONLXB/1RV/Alexander RL Type H47/32F delivered new as SO18 in April 1987 and was seen here in storage at Dundee depot. It would later be renumbered as 918 and remained in service into Stagecoach days as its fleet number 14685.

WLT 921 was an AEC Routemaster R2RH/Park Royal H36/28R new as London Transport RM921 in November 1961. It was purchased by Strathtay in July 1986 and numbered as its SR8. It was allocated to Dundee and is shown laying over between runs. It would lose its registration number in favour of YTS 892A in August 1987 as the company wanted to put the original plates onto its coach fleet to disguise the age of the vehicles.

EGB 73T was a Leyland Leopard PSU3E/3R/Alexander Y Type B53F new as Central Scottish T341 in January 1979. It became Kelvin Central Buses number 1473, before purchase by Strathtay in November 1995. It entered service in its previous livery of red and cream and carried fleet number 573.This view shows it working in Perth in full livery. It is currently being restored at Bridgeton bus museum in Glasgow.

In 1992 a pair of new Plaxton Paramount C49Ft Volvo B10Ms were purchased from dealer stock for upgrading the Scottish Citylink fleet. They were numbered as SV1/2, which was the second use of that sequence, originally used of Volvo Ailsa double-deckers. It was re-registered as VOH 640 in February 1998, and lasted into Stagecoach days as 52126. It passed to a dealer and was exported to Zimbabwe in April 2008.

Allocated to Perth, YMS 706R was a Volvo Ailsa B55-10/Alexander AV Type H44/35F new as Alexander (Midland) MRA6 in May 1977. It became Strathtay Scottish SV5 and is seen in Mill Street in Perth. It left the fleet in December 1991 when it passed to Kelvin Central Buses as its fleet number 1970, and was based at Old Kilpatrick and then Cumbernauld depot.

A987 FLS was a Leyland Olympian ONLXB/1R/Alexander RL Type H45/32F new as Fife Scottish FRO7 in November 1983. It would be renumbered as 787 before sale to Strathtay Scottish in 1988. This batch was refurbished by SBG Engineering at Kirkcaldy Works in 1989. Initially numbered as SO22 and re-registered as PSU 373, it would later become number 922. It was captured in Dundee, alongside a Tayside Volvo Ailsa.

Seagate, Dundee, is the location of this Strathtay Leyland Tiger TRBTL11/2R/Alexander P Type B52F. It had been new to Northern Scottish as NBT12 in 1983 and was based in the Buchan area. Four of these early Tigers were transferred to Strathtay in 1987 in exchange for Leyland Nationals, which were to be initially used on Perth City services. This one is seen after its second re-paint by Strathtay, with the paint scheme disguising the rather box-like style of the P Type – a design originally destined for the Singapore Market.

VLT 45 was an AEC Routemaster/Park Royal H36/28R purchased new by London Transport as its RM45 in September 1959. On disposal in February 1988 it joined Strathtay Scottish, and was later re-registered as AST 415A. This view shows it running in Dundee, looking rather strange with parts from other buses added to it. It was sold to Reading Mainline as its number 12 in June 1994 and withdrawn in 2000. It was then bought by London Buses and refurbished, re-entering service in December 2002.

YSF 80S was a Leyland Leopard PSU3D/4R/Alexander Y Type B53F new as Alexander (Fife) FPE80 in August 1977. It passed to Strathtay ten years later and was given fleet number SL57, as shown in this view taken in Dundee. It was transferred to Roadcar in September 1992 and ran for around seven more years. The white waistband improved the livery drastically.

D817 EES was a Leyland Olympian ONLXB/1RV/Alexander RL Type H47/32F that was new as Strathtay Scottish SO17 in April 1987. The white waistband was added to the livery in February 1988, as shown by this shot, taken in Dundee. It was later renumbered as 917 and had coach seats fitted. It became Stagecoach number 14684 in July 2006 after the Yorkshire Traction Group sold the business.

XSS 39Y was a Leyland Leopard PSU3G/4R/Alexander Y Type B53F new as Northern Scottish NPE39 in December 1982. It would receive number 539 in the renumbering scheme executed in March 1993. Alexander Coachbuilders supplied the Scottish Bus Group with a total of 2,729 Y Types, making it the most common type on the roads of Scotland.

VSS 1X was a Leyland Tiger TRCTL11/3R/Duple Goldliner III C46Ft purchased new by Northern Scottish in July 1982 for use on the Aberdeen to London service. The type was originally codenamed as the B43 before the Tiger name was chosen by Leyland Motors in 1980. It offered more power than the earlier Leopards with a 218 bhp output, utilising the turbocharged TL11H engine, and had air suspension.

CRS 67T was a Leyland Leopard PSU3E/4R/Alexander T Type C49F purchased new by Alexander (Northern) as its NPE67 in March 1979. It passed to Strathtay Scottish as its SL26, and later became 526. It gained the registration plate YSV 318 in 1988, and is seen in Dundee while working on the 40X service, which came into the city from Montrose.

M21 UUA was a Dennis Lance 11SDA/Optare Sigma B47F built as a demonstrator for Optare, Crossgates, in August 1994. It was inspected by Strathtay in 1995, and is shown at Dundee. It was used by Felix of Stanley between 1995 and 2000, then Chester's of Walkden as VOI 2412 and finally by O'Falluin of Dublin as 94-D-51682.

Shown at Montrose, M954 XES was a Volvo Olympian YN2RV/Northern Counties CH43/29F new as Strathtay Scottish 954 in May 1995. It would remain into Stagecoach days as number 16884, and later passed into preservation at Dundee Museum of Transport. This style of bodywork was known as the Palatine II, and was launched in 1993, only to be superseded by the Plaxton President in 1997.

C259 FGG was a Leyland Tiger TRCLXC/2RH/Alexander TE Type C49F new as Central Scottish LT59 in August 1985. It became Kelvin Central Buses 2277 in July 1989, but was almost immediately resold to Strathtay Scottish, where it would become ST20. January 1992 saw it become HSK 766, and it was renumbered as 420 the following year. It would become Stagecoach 59072 in July 2006.

E287 OMG was a Mercedes 709D/Reebur B25F purchased new by Tom Jowitt of Tankersley as its M3 in March 1988. The operation was taken over by Yorkshire Traction through its Barnsley & District subsidiary in July 1990. This bus was transferred to Roadcar in May 1991, then joined Strathtay in March 1999 as fleet number 166. It is shown in Dundee, and would become Stagecoach 40178 in July 2006.

SSA 8X was a Leyland Olympian ONLXB/1R/Alexander RL Type H45/32F new as Northern Scottish NLO8 in October 1981. It passed to Strathtay in 1985, becoming SO1 and later 901. December 1995 saw it withdrawn after an accident, but it returned to service with an ECW-style front dash panel. It lasted long enough to become Stagecoach 14680 in 2006. It was re-registered as MSL 466X on disposal to allow the SSA plate to be reused.

B133 PMS was a Leyland Tiger TRCTL11/3RH/Duple Laser 2 C46Ft new as Midland Scottish MPT133 in April 1985. It passed to Strathtay two months later, becoming ST10. November 1988 saw the VLT45 marque applied and it is shown at Arbroath. It would become number 410 and be re-seated to C57F in due course. The Scottish Bus Group purchased a total of twenty Duple Laser coaches.

LMS 168W was a Leyland Fleetline FE30AGR/Alexander D Type H75F new as Midland Scottish MRF168 in September 1980. It passed to Strathtay Scottish as its SD16 in June 1985 with Midland's Perth operations, but was caught operating in Dundee later in its life as number 716. It is now preserved in Midland livery, and owned by Messers Conn & Gurr.

LJA 476P was a Daimler Fleetline CRG6LXB/Northern Counties H43/32F new as Greater Manchester PTE 7476 in January 1976. It was acquired by Strathtay Scottish as its SD17 in March 1987, and renumbered to 717 in March 1993. It was captured working in Perth. On disposal it passed to Andrews of Sheffield, another company that came into the Yorkshire Traction fold. In June 1983, Greater Manchester Transport purchased a 49 per cent shareholding in the coachbuilder, but by May 1991 it was placed in administration.

V317 DSL was a Dennis Dart SPD/East Lancs DP43F new as Strathtay 317 in November 1999, and was based at Blairgowrie depot. It is shown at Seagate in Dundee, working on service 78C, bound for Monikie. It would become Stagecoach 33267 in July 2006 and had 'Tayway' branding applied. Sadly, it was lost in a fire in 2010.

T167 ATS was a Mercedes O814D/Plaxton Beaver DP25F new as Strathtay number 167 in May 1999. It received this special livery for operating to Dundee Airport. It received Stagecoach fleet number 42237 in 2006, and was fitted with an LED destination display in 2011. It later passed to the Souter Foundation in 2014 as a non-PSV.

NLS 988W was a Leyland National NL116L11/1R B52F new as Midland Scottish MPN36 in December 1980. It passed to Strathtay with Perth depot in 1985 as its SN8, and was caught in Mill Street. It was sold to Northern Scottish as its NPN18 in April 1987, then moved to Fife Scottish as its number 388 in December 1989. It passed to Stagecoach with that business and later moved to Ribble. Roadcar purchased it in December 1997 and ran it until 2003.

C261 FGG was a Leyland Tiger TRCLX/2RH/Alexander TE Type C49F purchased new in September 1985. LT61 would later don Monklands Bus livery very briefly before the company was merged with Kelvin Scottish to form Kelvin Central Buses, where it became 2279. It was quickly sold to Strathtay Scottish, where it became ST22 with registration number HSK 792. It survived into Stagecoach days as number 59073.

RLS 468T was a Ford R1014/Alexander Y Type B45F purchased new by Midland Scottish as its fleet number MT68 in January 1979. It was transferred to Strathtay in June 1985, and was caught in Perth. On disposal it passed to Meredith of Malpas, Owen's of Rhiwlas and WJC Coaches of Airdrie. Sister bus RLS 469T has been preserved in Strathtay colours.

TGM 233J was a Daimler Fleetline CRG6LXB/ECW H43/34F new as Central SMT D33 in June 1971. The type was not popular and it was quickly disposed of to Alexander (Northern) in January 1976, where it became NRF11. At one point the Scottish Bus Group had even offered them to Bristol Omnibus. Strathtay SD2 is seen in Montrose town centre.

EGB 70T was a Leyland Leopard PSU3E/3R/Alexander Y Type B53F new as Central Scottish T338 in January 1979. It became Kelvin Central Buses number 1470 in 1989, and passed to Strathtay in November 1995. It retained KCB livery for a spell, but was eventually repainted into fleet livery. It later worked for the associated Meffan of Kirriemuir fleet.

GLS 951V was a Leyland Leopard PSU3F/4R/Duple Dominant II Express C49F purchased new by Midland Scottish as its MPE 371 in May 1980. It passed to Strathtay with Perth depot and had the side mouldings changed to match the paint job. SL33 would later be re-registered to 821 DYE, but this was changed to ESN 700V on disposal to allow the cherished plate to be retained by the company.

A113 ESA was a Leyland Tiger TRBTL11/2R/Alexander P Type B52F new as Northern Scottish NBT13 in September 1983. The Scottish Bus Group purchased twenty-seven examples of this rather box-like design, which used flat glass throughout. Strathtay acquired four of this type, which were helped by the straight-line livery style employed.

SP51 AWV was a Volvo B7TL/East Lancs Vyking H47/29F new as Strathtay 701 in November 2001. It was one of three purchased to upgrade the 'Tayway' services, built to low-height spec in order to fit under the bridge at Inverkeilor. It passed to Stagecoach as its 16921 in 2006, and was re-registered as WLT427. On disposal it passed to Connexions Buses in Harrogate.

TSO 28X was a Leyland Olympian ONLXB/1R/ECW H45/32F new as Northern Scottish NLO28 in March 1982. It passed to Strathtay in June 1985 as fleet number S010. It briefly carried this advert for NORCO, which was originally the Northern Co-Operative Society Limited, but the lettering was soon removed after NORCO failed. The bus passed to the associated Roadcar fleet in October 1998, then Johnson's of Hodthorpe in June 2004.

E664 UNE was a Volvo B10M-61/Plaxton Paramount 3500 C53F new as Smith Shearings number 664 in January 1988. It passed to Yorkshire Traction in November 1992 as its number 51, and was re-registered as RHE 194. It became E769 AHL before transfer to Strathtay, but this was immediately changed to WLT 610, as shown in this view taken in Edinburgh.

USO 166S was a Ford R1114/Alexander Y Type B53F new as Alexander (Northern) NT166 in November 1977. It became Strathtay SF12 in 1985, and was photographed in Arbroath. The Fords were lightweight vehicles and not as durable as the Leylands which replaced them. A total of 273 Alexander Y Types were built on Ford chassis.

JLS 764S was a Ford R1014/Duple Dominant Express C45F new as Alexander (Midland) MT64 in July 1978. It is shown as Strathtay SF11 in Mill Street in Perth, and ran until withdrawal in 1987. It passed to Grangeburn Coaches of Motherwell, then moved to MacDonald of Howmore the following year.

BSG 546W was a Leyland Tiger TRCTL11/3R/Duple Dominant III C46Ft new as Eastern Scottish XH 546 in July 1981. It passed to Midland Scottish and then Kelvin Scottish before passing to Strathtay as its ST17 in July 1986. It was re-registered as 17 CLT and was rebuilt to Dominant IV spec the following year. It then became XDS 685W, and then 821 DYE. It was rebodied by East Lancs in May 1992 and ran until 2004.

G896 FJW was Renault S56/Dormobile B25F new as Strathtay Scottish SS13 in August 1989. It is seen here in Montrose as number 113. This batch was delivered in red to match the Perth City Transport-liveried Routemasters, but had 'City Nipper' fleet names. Dormobile had its roots in the Martin Walker business, located at the Dormobile works in Folkstone.

P367 UUG was Volvo B10B-58/Wright Endurance DP49F new as Harrogate & District number 367 in December 1996. It was acquired by Strathtay in March 2004 and allocated fleet number 611, as shown in this view taken in Dundee. It would pass to Stagecoach as its number 20020 in July 2006. The Volvo B10BLE featured a Volvo DH10A engine with a displacement of 9,600cc. An inline four-stroke six-cylinder diesel with a turbocharger and intercooler, it has a power output of either 245 or 285 bhp.

P311 HSN was a Dennis Dart SLF/East Lancs B39F new as Strathtay number 311 in November 1996, seen working on service 16 in Dundee. It would remain in the fleet until 2009 under Stagecoach ownership as number 33261. In 2008 the owner of East Lancs, Jamesstan Investments, controlled by the Darwen Group, purchased bus manufacturer Optare. Later, in June 2008, a reverse takeover was performed, with the Darwen name disappearing in favour of Optare's.

BAJ 637Y was a Leyland Tiger TRCTL11/3R/Plaxton Paramount 3500 C49Ft purchased new by Trimdon Motor Services in May 1983. It passed through many operators and has carried many registration plates – including 2090 VT, DFP 492Y, MIA 2032 and YOI 139 – before becoming DBZ 918 with Baldwin's of Sheffield. It passed through Yorkshire Terrier and Andrew's of Sheffield before purchase by Strathtay in September 1999. Purchased for rebodying, this was done by East Lancs in June 2000.

C262 FGG was a Leyland Tiger TRCLXC/2RH Alexander TE Type C49F purchased new by Central Scottish as its LT62 in September 1985. Central was embroiled in industrial action after management tried to impose new conditions on the staff. Sadly, even more industrial action followed and it was decided to close part of the company down and merge the rest with Kelvin Scottish in 1989. C262 FGG was also a casualty and moved to Strathtay Scottish at the same time, where it was numbered ST23 and re-registered to WLT 784.

These Daimler Fleetline CRL6-30/Alexander H74Ds were purchased new by Aberdeen Corporation in March 1973, then became owned by Grampian. They passed to Northern Scottish as NRF 142–4 and were used in the Aberdeen area, but in May 1985 I saw them in Perth carrying Midland Scottish legal lettering with a fleet number on the rear, which had been changed to MRF 142–4. I don't believe that this was ever recorded but about a week later they had passed to Strathtay Scottish and became SD7–9.

G293 MWU was a Renault S75/Reebur DP31F new as Harrogate & District number 293 in April 1990. It passed to Strathtay in June 1993 as its number 204, and was spotted in Perth working on service 58. It later worked for the associated Roadcar fleet in Lincolnshire as its number 153, before disposal to Briggs of Crymlyn Burrows in 2002.

WLT 316 had begun life as Midland Scottish ULS 650T, and was a Leyland Leopard PSU3E/4R/ Duple Dominant II C49F purchased new in March 1979 as MPE 343. It was transferred to Kelvin Scottish as E343, later becoming 3043 in June 1985, and moved to Strathtay in 1988. It was re-registered as WLT 316 using the plate from ex-London Routemaster SR25, which then became WTS 333A.

YHE 236J was a Leyland Leopard PSU3B/4R/Alexander Y Type C49F new as Yorkshire Traction number 236 in May 1971. It was cut down at Barnsley Works to serve as a tow-wagon in October 1991, and transferred to Strathtay Scottish. It was allocated fleet number 96, and is shown at Dundee depot. It would pass to Stagecoach with the business and become number 25796 in the process.

Strathtay decided to rebrand some of its Metrobuses in coach livery in 1988, and these three were caught in Perth depot before entering service. They retained bus seats, however, at this stage. Notice the difference in the destination screens after the company decided to move away from the traditional SBG style triangular versions.

D278 FAS was a Leyland Tiger TRCTL11/3RH/Alexander TE Type C53F new as Highland Scottish Z278 in May 1987. The company was in financial difficulties and resold the bus within three months to Fife Scottish, where it became number FLT31. It passed to Stagecoach with the business and was renumbered as 478. Strathtay purchased it in May 2001 and it was allocated fleet number 438. It was re-registered to VLT45 two years later, and passed back into Stagecoach ownership in 2006. Happily it is now in preservation.

SHE 611Y was a Leyland Olympian ONLXB/1R/ECW H45/32F purchased new by Yorkshire Traction as its fleet number 611 in August 1982. It was sent on loan to Strathtay Scottish in April 2001, and was captured in Dundee. It was sent up to cover an emergency school contract, awarded after Morgan Academy suffered fire damage. It would return to Yorkshire a year later.

ASA 21T was a Leyland Fleetline FE30AGR/ECW H43/32F new as Northern Scottish NRF21 in November 1978. It passed to Strathtay Scottish in June 1985 as its SD13 and was allocated to Blairgowrie depot. It was re-registered as YSR 152T in March 1990, and renumbered to 713 three years later.

VLT 191 was an AEC Routemaster R2RH/Park Royal H36/28R new as London Transport RM191 in February 1960. It was acquired by Strathtay in March 1987 as its SR22. It spent time on loan to Kelvin Scottish, then Highland Scottish, where it would be re-registered as AST 416A. It returned in 1989 and was renumbered as 622. On disposal it passed to Reading Mainline before returning to the capital with Transport for London.

P452 BPH was a Dennis Lance 11SDA/Northern Counties Paladin B49F built in October 1996 as a demonstrator for Plaxton's of Scarborough. It ran for Strathtay in February and March 2000, and was seen here working in Dundee. It would later find a permanent home with the Birmingham Coach Company/Diamond Bus and the Green Transport Company.

VRS 143L was a Daimler Fleetline CRL6-30/Alexander AL Type H45/29D new as Aberdeen Corporation number 143 in March 1973. It passed through the hands of Grampian Regional Transport before disposal. It worked for Northern Scottish, then Midland Scottish for around a week before it was transferred to Strathtay Scottish as its SD8. It was then purchased by Highland Scottish before being acquired by McKindless of Wishaw.

Seen working in Dundee, SP03 GDU was a Volvo B7TL/East Lancs Vyking H47/29F new as Strathtay number 711 in May 2003. It would become Stagecoach number 16931 in July 2006 and receive 'Tayway' branding. Stagecoach Strathtay was later put under the control of Stagecoach Fife.

296 HFM was a Bristol Lodekka LD6G/ECW H33/27RD new as Crosville DLG 960 in December 1958. It later worked for Walkers Coaches of Anderton before arriving at Strathtay as a driver training vehicle in 1986. It is shown at Dundee as ACA 230A and was allocated fleet number SDTV1. Note the vents for the Cave-Brown-Cave heating system on either side of the destination screen aperture.

CRS 72T, a Leyland Leopard PSU3E/4R/Duple Dominant Express C49F new as Alexander Northern Scottish NPE72 in August 1979, is seen arriving in Aberdeen on the 101 service from Dundee. It joined Strathtay in June 1985 as fleet number SL27, and was re-registered as 691 DYE in 1987. It received registration plate ASP 218T in 1992, and was renumbered as 527 in March 1993.

XMS 501K was a Daimler Fleetline CRG6LXB/Alexander D Type H44/31F new as Alexander (Midland) MRF101 in October 1971. It passed to Strathtay as its SD6 and is shown in Perth depot. It had a short life with the company and was sold to Wood's of Great Longstone in 1987, then Guide Friday in September 1989.

C241 OFE was a Mercedes L608D/Reebur DP19F new as Lincolnshire Roadcar number 41 in July 1986. It was transferred to Strathtay in July 1994 and allocated fleet number 134. It was loading outside the St John Centre in Perth for a journey to Blairgowrie. It would last with the company for ten years.

R453 MSL was a Volvo B10M-62/Plaxton Profile C49Ft that was new as Strathtay 453 in October 1997 for Scottish Citylink duties. It was re-registered as 143 CLT in June 2006 and allocated Stagecoach fleet number 52433 the following month. It received an LED destination screen and was allocated to Megabus work from Perth depot. On disposal it moved to Hughes Bros (t/a Alpine Travel) of Llandudno.

TSO 25X was a Leyland Olympian ONLXB/1R/ECW H45/32F new as Northern Scottish NLO25 in March 1982. It became Strathtay Scottish SO7, later 907, and was seen passing through Dundee, complete with a conductor beside the driver. It was transferred to the associated Roadcar fleet as its 625 in March 1999.

GYS 77X was a Mercedes L508D/Pilcher Greene DP16F purchased new by the Jewish Association for the Mentally Handicapped, Glasgow, in June 1982. It was acquired by Strathtay Scottish as its SS5 in August 1989, and was snapped in Perth, outside the Sandeman Building in Kinnoull Street. This used to be a library, but it is a pub nowadays.

DLS 257S was a Ford R1114/Duple Dominant Express C49F new as Alexander (Midland) MT57 in August 1977. It passed to Strathtay, and has had the fleet names altered. It became SF7 and ran until November 1987, when it passed to Grangeburn of Motherwell. It then moved to Docherty of Motherwell in 1988 and Cleland of Newarthill the following year.

WLT 943, which started life as D315 SGB, was a Duple 340-bodied Leyland Tiger that was new to Central Scottish. It was rebodied by East Lancs for Strathtay in July 2000, and was on a hire to Hampden Park in Glasgow when captured. It passed to Stagecoach with the business, and was sold to Woottens/Tiger Line where it became B11 WTN. It then passed to McCree of Shepshed & Ogden of St Helens for further service, latterly as AAL 520A.

D570 VBV was a Freight Rover Sherpa 374/Dormobile B16F new as Ribble 570 in November 1986. On disposal in May 1988 it was acquired by Roadcar as its number 70. It moved to Strathtay in August 1991, and is shown in Perth depot as number SS27, but later became number 127. It would later transfer to the Meffan of Kirriemuir fleet for further service in 1995.

A busy scene taken at Crieff depot in 1988 shows a variety of the fleet then allocated there. All were based on Leyland Leopard chassis, with three carrying Alexander coachwork and one bodied by Duple. The service buses came from Fife and Midland Scottish. Note that all three have different front end variations in the grille area. The coach was originally GLS 948V in the Midland fleet.

XMS 424Y was a Leyland Leopard PSU3G/4R/Alexander Y Type B53F new as Midland Scottish MPE 424 in November 1982. It passed to Strathtay Scottish with Perth depot in June 1985, and was allocated fleet number SL46. It later became 546 and had yellow added to the livery, but it has been said that this was not sanctioned by head office. It became 25574 in Stagecoach days, and later passed to Keenan of Coalhall for further service.

S342 SWF was a Mercedes O814D/Plaxton Beaver B31F new as Yorkshire Traction number 342 in September 1998. It joined Strathtay in 2006 as number 227, and was allocated to Dundee depot. It would receive Stagecoach fleet number 42227 in July 2006, and remain in the fleet until 2009.

G56 RGG was a Volvo B10M-60/Plaxton Paramount III 3500 C53F purchased new by Park's of Hamilton in March 1990. It passed to Fishwick's of Leyland in March 1992, then Greater Manchester South in April 1995, Jones of Market Drayton in 1996 and Moore of Davenport in 1997. It was hired by Strathtay in June 1997, and was caught here in Glasgow. It moved to Tourist Coaches as USV 115, then Barry's of Weymouth as G56 RGG once again.

YMS 701R was a Volvo Ailsa B55-10/Alexander AV Type H44/35F new as Alexander (Midland) MRA1 in May 1977. It passed to Strathtay in June 1985 and was allocated to Perth depot. It moved to Dundee in September 1989, and ran there until sale to Kelvin Central Buses as its number 1980 the following year. It was working on service 77, bound for Gauldry, when seen.

ULS 648T was a Leyland Leopard PSU3E/4R/Duple Dominant II C49F purchased new by Midland Scottish as its MPE 341 in April 1979. It was transferred to Strathtay Scottish in June 1985, and was heading to unload tour passengers at Fisher's Hotel in Pitlochry when photographed. Incidentally, the hotel was owned by the former directors of Greyhound Coaches of Dundee.

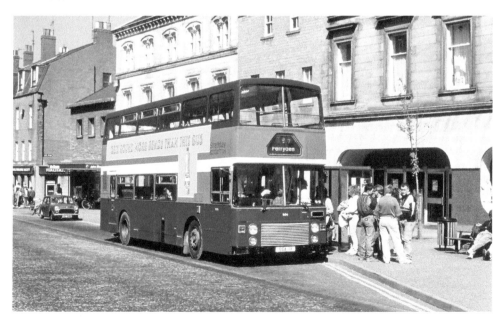

SSA 11X was a Leyland Olympian ONXLB/1R/Alexander RL Type H45/32F purchased new by Northern Scottish as its NLO11 in October 1981. It was transferred to Strathtay Scottish in June 1985 as number SO4, but was later renumbered as 804. This shot was taken in Montrose, and shows the bus loading for the Ferryden service.

E414 GES was an MCW Metrobus DR102/60/Alexander RL Type H47/33F new as Strathtay Scottish SM14 in August 1987. It was given this livery in 1988, and was re-registered as YJU 694 in 1993. This view shows it in Dundee as fleet number 814. It would be allocated Stagecoach number 15894, and leave the fleet in 2007.

CRS 75T was a Leyland Leopard PSU3E/4R/Duple Dominant Express C49F new as Northern Scottish NPE75 in August 1979. It is shown in Dundee just after the takeover, and would become SL20 in due course. It later gained 'Mackays Coaches' colours to compete with Smith's of Coupar Angus, and was given the dateless registration number YJU 694. It would later become number 528 and retire as ASP 97T.

ULS 633X was an MCW Metrobus DR102/28/Alexander RL Type H45/33F new as Midland Scottish MRM33 in May 1982. Strathtay inherited eight of these buses, with a further three on order. SM5 was a Perth bus, but moved to Dundee after Perth depot closed in 1990. The white band was added to the livery in April 1989, and greatly improved the look of the fleet.

T167 ATS was a Mercedes O814D/Plaxton Beaver DP25F purchased new by Strathtay in May 1999 for use on the Dundee Airport service. It is shown in fleet livery while working on a local Dundee service. It would become Stagecoach number 42237, and had an LED destination fitted to replace roller blinds fitted in 2011.

135 D819 EES was a Leyland Olympian ONLXB/1RV/Alexander RL Type H47/32F new as Strathtay Scottish SO19 in April 1987. It gained the white waistband in 1989, and was captured here arriving in Dundee. It was fitted with coach seats in 1998, and remained into Stagecoach days as number 14686.

DMS 20V was a Leyland National NL116L11/1R B52F new as Midland Scottish MPN20 in February 1980. It became Strathtay Scottish SN1, and is shown freshly outshopped at Perth depot. It was later transferred to Northern Scottish as its NPN20, then Fife Scottish as number 380. It passed into Stagecoach ownership and later saw service with Red & White.

R522 TWR was a Volvo B10BLE/Wright DP47F new as Keighley & District number 522 in April 1998. It was acquired by Strathtay in May 2005 and received fleet number 615, as shown in this view taken in Dundee. It later became Stagecoach Strathtay number 21126 and was re-registered as PSU 376 in 2006. It returned to its original plate before disposal to Docherty's of Auchterarder and McCulloch of Stoneykirk.

C816 BTS was a Leyland Royal Tiger Doyen C49Ft new as Strathtay Scottish ST16 in June 1986. It was re-registered as WLT 784 in September 1986, and is seen in Scottish Citylink livery. The registration was changed to C849 CSN for disposal in 1991. It had many further owners, including Arle of Shipton Oliffe, Smith of Peterlee and Averon of Bootle.

D438 XRS was a Leyland Tiger TRCTL11/2RH/Alexander TC Type C57F new as Northern Scottish NCT38 in July 1987. It became Stagecoach Bluebird number 452 and gained the registration plate LSK 548 in 1993, then D438 XRS in 1997, VLT 272 in 1998, and D982 BRS in 1999. It passed to Strathtay in 2001 and was re-registered as VLT 183. Ironically, it returned to Stagecoach with the business and was allocated fleet number 59079.

OWE 858R was a Bristol VRT/ECW H43/31F new as Yorkshire Traction number 858 in February 1977. Seven of these buses were sent to Strathtay in 1991 and allocated to Dundee and Forfar depots. It returned to Yorkshire the following year and ran for a further year before sale to Johnson's of Hodthorpe in September 1993.

LFE 777Y was a Leyland Tiger TRCTL11/3R/Plaxton Paramount 3500 C49Ft purchased new by Appleby's of Conisholme in May 1983. It was re-registered as 128 NNU in March 1987. It then passed to Clayton of Leicester, Wooliscroft of Matlock and Kingsman of Holbrook before reaching Yorkshire Traction in 1996. It later worked for Andrews and Barnsley & District before transfer to Strathtay in 2003, and was passing through Edinburgh when seen.

M951 XES was a Volvo Olympian YN2R/Northern Counties CH43/29F new as Strathtay Scottish number 951 in May 1995. It is shown in Dundee with an advert for Coors Beer, which was only applied to the one side. It would become Stagecoach 16881 in due course. On disposal it ran for Leyland of Fulwood and Lawrenson of Preston.

H129 AML was a Renault S75/Reebur B29F new as London Buses RB29 in October 1990. London Buses bought thirty-three of these, and they were allocated to Bow garage for use on routes 100, 276 and S2. RB29 was acquired by Strathtay in 1994 and allocated to Dundee depot as number 206. It was transferred to Roadcar in 1996 as its number 369, and later passed to Simms of Lincoln in 2002.

SP51 AWX was a Volvo B7TL/East Lancs Vyking H47/29F new as Strathtay 703 in November 2001, seen at in Dundee. It would pass to Stagecoach with the business in 2006 as fleet number 16923. On disposal it would join Connexionsbuses for further service. This was the double-deck version of the Spryte. It continued the long line of 'misspelt' names, which continued until the Scania OmniDekka. The name 'Vyking' was derived from the chassis being built in Sweden.

BLS 424Y was an MCW Metrobus DR102/33/Alexander RL Type H45/33F purchased new by Midland Scottish as its MRM46 in April 1983, and transferred to Strathtay in June 1985 as number SM6. Advertising was pasted on the lower panels to maximise revenue at this time.

S401 HVV was a Dennis Dart SLF/East Lancs Spryte B40F delivered new to Pete's Travel of West Bromwich in November 1998. It was lent to Strathtay between June and September 2000 to cover for warranty work. It later joined Yellow Buses in Bournemouth as its number 490. Note the conductor on the front platform.

G278 TSL was a Mercedes 709D/Alexander B23F new as Magicbus Glasgow number 278 in March 1990, but also served elsewhere within the group. It later passed to Docherty's of Auchterarder before joining Strathtay in 2003. It was initially number 184, but had become 40174 by the time this picture was taken at Arbroath, while under Stagecoach ownership.

N308 DSL was a Dennis Dart 9.8SDL/Northern Counties B39F new as Strathtay Scottish number 308 in January 1996. The coachbuilder was based in Wigan, and produced this style between 1991 and 1998. 308 would become Stagecoach 32906 for a spell before being sold to Eatonways of Ramsgate in 2009.

VSS 1X was a Leyland Tiger TRCTL11/3R/Duple Goldliner III C46Ft new as Northern Scottish NLT1 in July 1982. It became Strathtay ST1 in June 1986, and was caught passing through Durham on its way to Rugby. It was re-registered as WLT 610, then LTS93X on disposal to Tame Valley. It was snapped up by Midland Red North and sent to East Lancs for a new B61F body in 1992, echoing the similar ideas held by Strathtay themselves.

R958 TSL was a low-height Volvo Olympian-49/East Lancs Pyoneer CH72F purchased new by the company in March 1988. It passed to Stagecoach with the business in 2006 and was renumbered to 16812, with the registration being changed to HSK 792. The view shows it in Dundee, heading for Ninewells Hospital.

V20 CBC was a Mercedes O814D/Plaxton Beaver B31F purchased new by Coakley of Motherwell in January 2000. It was acquired by Ashall of Clayton in January 2002, but only lasted for four months before sale to Strathtay. 220 is shown in Montrose, outside the Scotmid store. It would become Stagecoach 42220, but suffered fire damage and went for scrap in 2007.

LJA 478P was a Daimler Fleetline CRG6LXB/Northern Counties H43/32F new as Greater Manchester PTE number 7478 in February 1976. It was acquired by Strathtay Scottish in February 1987 and allocated fleet number SD19, and later 719. It was transferred to the Meffan fleet in 1993 and repainted as shown. It returned to Strathtay the following year, but was never repainted.

This Ford Transit/Deansgate B12F was new as ERE 858N to Crystal Coaches, but was rebuilt after an accident by Stevenson's of Uttoxeter and re-registered as ORE 830W. It was purchased by Strathtay in July 1988 and allocated fleet number SS2, as evident in this view taken at Blairgowrie depot.

D818 EES was a Leyland Olympian ONLXB/1RV/Alexander RL Type H47/32F new as Strathtay Scottish SO18 in April 1987. It received this advertising livery in June 1994 and it was used to promote an anti-road rage campaign for Tayside Police. It was allocated to Arbroath depot at this time, and was snapped in Dundee. It became Stagecoach 14685 in July 2006.

Perth had its own municipal buses, but sold the thirty-five vehicles to W. Alexander & Sons in 1934. The crimson livery was retained for local services until 1961, when it was abandoned in favour of Alexander azure blue. Strathtay decided to resurrect the identity after Stagecoach decided to compete on local services. A line-up of AEC Routemasters sits in Perth depot in June 1989.

YN55 KND was an Optare Solo M880 B27F new as Strathtay number 259 in October 2005. This was the penultimate vehicle delivered to Strathtay under Yorkshire Traction ownership. It gained Stagecoach fleet number 47259 in July 2006. As this was the standard small bus for both Strathtay and Stagecoach, it did not stand out once it donned Stagecoach livery.

K303 MSN was a Dennis Dart 9.8SDL/Wright Handybus B39F new as Strathtay Scottish number 303 in April 1993. It was working a local route in Arbroath when seen. It received Stagecoach number 32478 in due course, along with branding for Arbroath town services, and remained in service until 2008. The Traction Group often utilised smaller bodybuilders, where they could exert a greater influence.

SHE 611Y was a Leyland Olympian ONLXB/1R/ECW H45/32F new as Yorkshire Traction number 611 in August 1982. It had been on loan to Strathtay in 2001, and returned to Yorkshire. It returned for a second time in July 2002, and was fully repainted in fleet livery, as shown by this view taken in Montrose.

C114 JCS was a Leyland Tiger TRCLXC/2RH/Duple 320 C49Ft new as Central Scottish C14 in April 1986. It passed to Strathtay via Kelvin Central Buses in May 1990 as ST24. It was re-registered as WLT 610, as shown in this view taken in Glasgow. It was re-registered as C23 MAK on disposal in 1995 and was exported to Eire as 86-K-1396 after a succession of UK owners.

The company acquired a staggering range of one-off buses, often from non-PSV owners. M289 XSF was a Mercedes 814D/TBP B20FL which came from BLESMA Home in Crieff in March 2002. It was given fleet number 183 and is seen in Dundee. TBP bodies were built by Turner Brown Precision Engineering at Bilston, near Wolverhampton.

ULS 627X was an MCW Metrobus DR102/28/Alexander RL Type H45/33F new as Midland Scottish MRM27 in May 1982. MCW introduced the Metrobus after Leyland announced that it would build complete buses. The Metrobus was available as a complete vehicle or a chassis. The Scottish Bus Group got Alexander to provide the bodywork and the spec included air brakes, a Voith gearbox and a retarder.

Blairgowrie bus depot was located in Haugh Road, and this view taken from the entrance shows a cross-section of the buses allocated there: Metrobuses, a Fleetline, a Leopard, a Mercedes and a Renault minibus are all visible. Nowadays, Stagecoach provides all the bus services to and from Blairgowrie with routes to Perth, Dundee, Alyth, Coupar Angus, Dunkeld, Aberfeldy, Kirkmichael and Glenshee, as well as a circular town service.

Perth depot had an allocation of Daimler and Leyland Fleetlines. Two ex-Midland examples, acquired when the Scottish Bus Group was re-organised in 1985, sit between two ex-Manchester examples which were supplied second-hand by Kirkby (dealer) of Anston in 1987. The Fleetline was the SBG standard decker for many years, with a total of 640 being bought new.

Some of the Arbroath town services were operated by Greyhound Coaches, and more were registered on de-regulation. Strathtay also registered them, and Greyhound withdraw from stage carriage work in favour of the larger company. Dennis Dart 303 is seen in the town, wearing the later version of the livery.

D817 EES was a Leyland Olympian ONLXB/1RV/Alexander RL Type H47/32F new as Strathtay Scottish SO17 in April 1987. It is shown as number 911, in the later version of the livery, as it heads for Dundee city centre. It was given coach seats in 1998, and lasted into Stagecoach days as number 14686.

SK52 USS was a Transbus Enviro 300 B44F built as a demonstrator for Transbus, Guildford, in December 2002. It was used by Dundee depot in June 2003, and was caught working on service 16. It would later pass to Reading Buses as its number 974, then Premiere of Nottingham as its number 3341, before moving to Silverdale of Nottingham.

RHN 951F was a Bristol Lodekka FLF6G/ECW H38/32F new as United L251 in March 1968. It was swapped with Eastern Scottish for a Bristol VRT, and later became a driver trainer with both Eastern and Central Scottish. It was acquired by Strathtay Scottish in March 1989 and was allocated fleet number SDT1, as shown in this view taken in Perth depot.

SP05 FKG was a Volvo B7TL/East Lancs Vyking H47/29F new as Strathtay number 713 in July 2005. It later became 16933 in the national Stagecoach fleet numbering series following the acquisition of the Yorkshire Traction Group. It is seen here in Dundee while working service 75, bound for Carnoustie.

E748 MSC was a Mercedes 709D/Alexander C25F purchased new by Davidson of Whitburn in June 1988. It then worked for Carr of Whitburn and Pugh of Clock Face before reaching Strathtay in June 1996. Numbered 145, it was seen in Arbroath. It received Stagecoach fleet number 40173 in in July 2006, but didn't last long.

The Bristol VRT had a very chequered history in Scotland. The Scottish Bus Group, and later Tayside Regional Council, found them so unreliable that they were all sold out of service after just a few years. Later on, Stagecoach, Lowland and Strathtay ran examples without too many problems; however, the Strathtay examples were only in the fleet for a short time to cover extra work.

S960 KSR was a Volvo Olympian-50/East Lancs Pyoneer CH43/29F new as Strathtay number 960 in November 1998. The design was based on the Leyland Olympian, but the chassis was modified so that Volvo's standard electrical system was used, as well as standard steering/'Z cam' braking systems. The early versions were offered with a Cummins L10 or Volvo TD102KF engine coupled to a Voith DIWA or ZF Ecomat gearbox. From late 1996, only the 9.6-litre Volvo D10A-245 Euro II engine with electronic diesel control was offered.

V316 DSL was a Dennis Dart SPD/East Lancs Spryte DP43F new as Strathtay number 316 in November 1999. It became Stagecoach number 33266 in 2006, was fitted with an LED destination screen and ran until 2011. It was sold to McColl's Coaches of Dumbarton, then passed to Gough Travel of Carluke, where it was re-registered as L777 GOT.

SP54 ENO was an Optare Solo M880 B25F new as Strathtay number 251 in October 2004. It had 'The Friendly Bus' applied to the sides after Dundee City Council obtained funding for a shoppers' service, which linked various sheltered housing schemes to their local supermarkets. It became Stagecoach number 27251 in 2006 after the takeover.

WLT 917 was an AEC Routemaster R2RH/Park Royal H36/28R new as London Transport RM917 in November 1961. It was purchased by Strathtay Scottish in June 1986, and allocated fleet number SR20. January 1988 saw it re-registered to WTS 102A, and shortly after this it was given its second repaint by the company. The new layout was more sympathetic to the lines on the bodywork.

E414 GES was an MCW Metrobus DR102/60/Alexander RL Type H47/33F new as Strathtay Scottish SM14 in August 1987. It was fitted from new with this improved destination layout and looks smart here as it travels through the Perthshire countryside. It received this livery in 1988, and was renumbered as 814 in 1993. It was given the cherished plate YJU 694 later in life, and lasted into Stagecoach days.

ASA 25T was a Leyland Fleetline FE30AGR/ECW H43/32F new as Northern Scottish NRF25 in November 1978. It passed to Strathtay Scottish as its SD14, but was later renumbered as 714, as shown in this view. It features the white waistband introduced to brighten up the livery. It was re-registered as AES 116T in September 1999 in preparation for disposal early in the new millennium.

R507 WRV was an Optare MetroRider MR15 B31F new as Tillingbourne of Cranleigh number 507 in February 1998. It was re-registered as TIL 7897 in 2001, but was sold off to a dealer after the company got into financial difficulties. Strathtay purchased it in May 2001 and allocated it fleet number 219. It was reunited with its original registration plate the following year, and lasted into Stagecoach days.

N107 GVS was a Volvo B10B-58/Wright Endurance B51F new as Sovereign Bus & Coach 107 in February 1996. It was one of a batch purchased from the Blazefield Group, and arrived in May 2004. It became Strathtay number 607 and was seen here passing through Dundee. It lasted into Stagecoach days, but was withdrawn after fire damage in 2007.

SCS 365M was a Leyland Leopard PSU3/3R/Alexander Y Type C49F new in March 1975 as Western SMT L2496. It was acquired by Strathtay Scottish in June 1985, and is seen in Dundee with just the 'Scottish' part of the fleet name. These buses were acquired to allow the lightweight Fords to be withdrawn, and typically only ran for a couple of years.

N149 DSL was an Optare MetroRider MR35 DP25F new as Strathtay Scottish 149 in January 1996. It is seen in Dundee while working on service 70. There were four of these neat little buses in this batch and they were withdrawn between 2008 and 2010. Service 70 linked the city centre with Craigie Huntley Road, and was operated by Dundee depot.